21st
Century
Skills Library

REAL WORLD SCIENCE

ANIMALS

Stuart P. Levine

Cherry Lake Publishing
Ann Arbor, Michigan

CHERRY LAKE
Publishing

Published in the United States of America by Cherry Lake Publishing
Ann Arbor, Michigan
www.cherrylakepublishing.com

Content Adviser: Laura Graceffa, middle school science teacher; BA degree in science, Vassar College; MA degrees in science and education, Brown University

Photo Credits: Cover and page 1, © Shvaygert Ekaterina/Shutterstock; page 4, © Shutterstock; page 6, © aliciah/Shutterstock; page 8, © Cathy Kiefer/Shutterstock; page 9, © aliciah/Shutterstock; page 10, © Charles Taylor/Shutterstock; page 12, © aliciah/Shutterstock; page 14, © Stephane106/Shutterstock; page 16, © Floridastock/Shutterstock; page 17, © Four Oaks/Shutterstock; page 19, © Chris Kruger/Shutterstock; page 20, © Kitch Bain/Shutterstock; page 23, © painless/Shutterstock; page 25, © Ryan M. Bolton/ Shutterstock; page 27, © Christian Musat/Shutterstock; page 28, © Christian Musat/ Shutterstock

Library of Congress Cataloging-in-Publication Data

Levine, Stuart P., 1968-
Animals / Stuart Levine.
    p. cm. — (Real world science)
ISBN-13: 978-1-60279-456-6
ISBN-10: 1-60279-456-1
1. Animals—Juvenile literature. I. Title. II. Series.

QL49.L386 2008
590–dc22   2008040802

---

*Cherry Lake Publishing would like to acknowledge the work of
The Partnership for 21st Century Skills.
Please visit* www.21stcenturyskills.org *for more information.*

TABLE OF CONTENTS

CHAPTER ONE

WHO'S WHO IN THE ANIMAL WORLD?

The grasshopper is just one of many thousands of animals found in the natural world.

How many different kinds of animals do you think live on earth?

Scientists have been studying animals for a long time. So far they have

named more than 1.7 million different kinds of life forms!

Not all of these life forms, or **species**, are animals. Some are plants.

Some are bacteria. Some are fungi. All of these other things are alive, too. But scientists have a lot of rules about what makes something an animal: An animal has to be able to move on its own. It also needs to eat food of some kind. Animals include everything from worms and eagles to houseflies and humans. Scientists have identified about 1.3 million kinds of animals alive today. And new animals are being discovered all the time.

REAL WORLD SCIENCE CHALLENGE

Mammals, reptiles, birds, fish, and amphibians are all very different groups of animals. Can you figure out which group the following animals belong to? You can use what you have learned here. Or you can look the animals up on the Internet or in a book to find out more about them.

- Iguana
- Great white shark
- Chicken
- Bat
- Tree frog

(Turn to page 29 for the answer)

Like other snakes, the boa constrictor belongs to the reptile group in the animal kingdom.

With so many different types of animals on earth, scientists need a way to keep track of them. They use a system created about 250 years ago. The creator was a Swedish scientist named Carl Linnaeus. Linnaeus observed animals. He saw the ways they were the same. He saw the ways they were different. He used this information to organize them into groups.

The animal kingdom includes many different groups. These groups of animals all have different features.

Insects are the largest group. They have six legs and bodies with three sections. Ants, grasshoppers, butterflies, and beetles are all insects.

Reptiles are another group. This group includes snakes, lizards, and turtles. A reptile is cold-blooded. This does not mean that their blood is actually cold. It just means that their bodies stay the same temperature as their surroundings. If it is hot outside, they are hot. If it is cold outside, they are cold. Reptiles also have scales. These scales cover their whole body.

Birds are a group too. All birds have feathers. Their feathers keep them warm on the ground or up in the cold sky. Most also have hollow bones, which makes them light enough to fly—well, most of them. An ostrich is one bird that cannot fly. These large African birds are too heavy. But they are fast runners.

One of the oldest species of animal on earth is also one of the strangest. The horseshoe crab has been around for nearly 500 million years! It is not really a crab. In fact it is most closely related to spiders. Just like a spider, it needs to shed its skin as it grows larger. This is called molting. By the time a horseshoe crab is fully grown, it has molted nearly 20 times. But the horseshoe crab is even more amazing. If it loses a leg, it can just grow a new one back. No wonder horseshoe crabs have been around for so long!

This big-eyed tree frog is an amphibian, a group of animals that begins life with gills instead of lungs.

The group known as amphibians includes frogs and salamanders. They start out using **gills** to breathe underwater when they are young. When they become adults, they grow legs and start to breathe through lungs.

Fish are another group. They breathe underwater their whole lives. Sharks are a special kind of fish. They don't have solid bones. Instead they have a more flexible skeleton. It is made of **cartilage**. This is the same material we have in our ears and noses.

Mammals are the smallest group of animals. They number only about 5,000 different kinds. Mammals include tigers, dogs, monkeys, and humans.

Like all mammals, the Sumatran tiger is warm-blooded and has fur (or hair as it's called in humans.)

All mammals have hair. (We call it "fur" in animals other than humans.)

They are also warm-blooded. This means their bodies try to keep a constant temperature inside no matter what the outside temperature is.

There are so many types of animal in the world. They can be found almost everywhere on earth.

CHAPTER TWO

THERE'S NO PLACE LIKE HOME

A mother and baby orangutan make their home high up in the trees.

Most people live in a house or an apartment. Yours might be in a big

city. Or it might be in the country. It could be on a farm. Animals can live

in lots of different places too. The place an animal lives is called its **habitat**.

Each habitat has different places for animals to live. Some animals, such as birds and monkeys, live high up in the trees. Others, like wolves and deer, do better on the ground. There are even animals that live under the ground! Worms, many insects, and moles are examples of underground animals.

REAL WORLD SCIENCE CHALLENGE

Explore the habitats in your own backyard. Go outside and try to find an animal habitat. It can be a tree, a pond, a bush, or even a grassy field. Spend some time watching your habitat and write down what animals you see living there. Don't forget to include insects! Think about why they live in one type of habitat and not another. Try this at different times of the day and see what you find.

(Turn to page 29 for the answer)

Why do these animals all live in such different places? Each habitat only has a certain amount of food. If all the animals lived in the treetops,

A clown fish hides among sea anemones. These fish need saltwater to survive so they live in the ocean.

they would not have enough to eat. Animals usually fill up all the available spaces in a habitat. Each species finds a spot that has the right kind of food and shelter for it.

Not all animals live in the same kind of habitat. Clown fish, for example, need saltwater. So they live in the ocean. Lizards need a lot of heat. So they might live in a desert. Oceans and deserts are examples of **ecosystems**.

An ecosystem is the type of habitat an animal lives in. It is a community of living and non-living things within that habitat. Many species of plants and animals may live in an ecosystem. The ecosystem also includes water, rocks, and even weather! All of these these things are connected. Whatever happens to one part of an ecosystem can affect all the others.

A desert ecosystem seems like a very difficult place to live. It is hot and dry. There is very little to eat. Yet lots of animals survive just fine in the desert. The Mexican beaded lizard is one example. It is a

People build a lot of houses, roads, stores, and other things. Sometimes this takes space away from the animals that used to live there. Try putting up a bird bath in your yard. All you need is a large, shallow container for water. Birds need a place to wash their feathers each day. Do you live near water? If so, you can also make a home for frogs and toads. Cut a medium-sized notch in the lip of a flower pot or plastic container. Turn it upside down and place it outside. This little "cave" makes the perfect home for a frog. Some people even build bat boxes. You can find instructions on the Internet. The bats will fly inside and enjoy their cozy home.

*Animals that live in the desert have developed ways of
coping with extreme heat and little water.*

reptile. So it needs a lot of heat to stay warm and keep its body working.

It has tough skin that does not get sunburned. Mexican beaded lizards can

also go for days without water.

Some mammals can live in the desert as well. Fennec foxes are the

smallest members of the dog family. These tiny, golden-haired foxes are great diggers. They dig underground burrows. This is where they spend most of the hot desert days. At night they come out to find food. They look for small lizards, insects, birds, and even desert berries.

Tundra is another type of ecosystem. The ground in a tundra is almost always frozen. There is often snow on top of the ground. The temperature stays very low all year long. One animal that survives well in this ecosystem is the polar bear. Polar bears have a thick coat of fur. They also have a layer of fat to help keep them warm. The white color of their fur also has a purpose. It helps them blend in with the snow

21st Century Content

Some habitats are in danger. Forests are often cut down by people. All the animals that live there have to find a new place to live. Sometimes they cannot find a suitable new home. When that happens, they struggle to survive.

One such habitat is the rain forest of Borneo. Borneo is an island in Southeast Asia. People burn down the forests there to make room for palm tree farms. The oil from the palm fruit is used in many foods. It is also used for makeup and other beauty products. More than half of the forest has been burned down now. Apes called orangutans are one animal that live in Borneo's forests. These apes have nowhere else to go. They may not survive.

Polar bears have a layer of fat and thick fur to help them survive in the freezing temperatures of their habitat.

and ice. Polar bears spend most of their time near the icy water, looking

for their favorite food: seals!

Almost every place on earth can have some kind of animal living in it.

CHAPTER THREE

What's for Dinner?

An elephant reaches into a tree with its trunk for a tasty meal of bark and leaves.

Everyone has a favorite food. Many people also have foods they won't eat. Animals can be picky eaters too. **Herbivores** are animals that eat only plants. **Carnivores** are animals that eat only other animals. **Omnivores** are animals that eat both plants and animals. Humans are omnivores. Our bodies allow us to eat both kinds of food.

There are more herbivores in the world than carnivores. This is because the world has more plants than animals. Also, it is easier to feed on plants than on other animals. Plants make energy from the sun, air, and water. Herbivores eat the plants and take in that energy. This is how herbivores survive. Then carnivores eat the herbivores and take in their energy. This is known as the **food chain.**

One thing almost all herbivores have in common is a good sense of smell. This helps them find their food. Some plant eaters, like elephants, will travel many miles in search of one type of tree that they like to eat.

Giraffes use their long necks and long tongues to reach the leaves on the tops of trees.

Once they find their food of choice, they use all the tools that nature has given them. These "tools" are known as **adaptations**. They are the physical features or abilities that help the animal survive in its habitat. Elephants will reach up with their trunk to tear off tree branches. If they cannot reach the branch they want, they will use their large body to knock the tree over. Giraffes have long tongues that can reach lengths of over 18 inches (46 cm)! They wrap that long, flexible

Like many carnivores, the lion uses sharp teeth and claws to catch its prey.

tongue around leaves the same way that we close our hands around a

piece of food. Fruit bats will usually chew a piece of fruit until they have

sucked out all the juice. Then they spit out what is left over.

Carnivores are **predators**. This means they hunt for their food.

The animals they hunt are called their **prey**. The prey is usually an herbivore or an omnivore. Sometimes it could be another carnivore. Predators have to work very hard for their food. They have adaptations too. These special features help them catch their prey. A cheetah, for instance, can run very fast. It can catch a small antelope by chasing it down. Tigers, on the other hand, are not as fast as the food they chase. They must rely on their great strength and their ability to remain quiet. They sneak up on their prey, and once they get close, they pounce on it. Tigers have sharp claws and teeth, as well as powerful jaws. Once they catch their prey, they do not let it go.

Learning & Innovation Skills

Bats have an unusual way of hunting. Most bats eat flying insects. As a bat flies, it sends out a high-pitched noise. If a bug flies by, the noise will bounce off it. Bats have very sharp hearing. The bat can hear that sound bouncing off the bug. The bat keeps following the echoes to zero in on its prey and catch the bug. Other bats eat fruit. Actually, they only like the juice. They chew on the fruit and suck out all the juice. Then they spit out the skin and the seeds. The seeds fall to earth and help to replant new trees and plants.

Some predators use keen eyesight to catch their prey. Hawks often sit on top of telephone poles to watch for their prey. Even from this height, they can see a tiny mouse running through the grass. Once they spot it, they dive down and grab it with their sharp claws.

REAL WORLD SCIENCE CHALLENGE

Most predators have special adaptations that help them catch their prey. Most prey animals also have adaptations that help them to escape predators. Make a list of all of the predators and prey you can think of. Or, use a book or the Internet to make your list. Try to think about the adaptations that help them both to survive. Look at pictures of their bodies and read about their behavior to get a few clues.

(Turn to page 29 for the answer)

Animals spend a large part of their lives looking for food. No matter where they live, they are all concerned about what is on the menu that day.

CHAPTER FOUR

LIFE CYCLES

With mouths wide open, baby birds signal their parents that they are ready to eat.

One thing all animals have in common is that they have babies.

Mammals carry their babies inside them. They give birth to live young.

Birds and many reptiles lay eggs instead. Their babies develop inside the

eggs, not in their bodies.

Birds spend many days or weeks building a nest. Once they lay their

eggs they sit on them for several more weeks. This keeps the eggs warm.

Most often the mother does the bulk of that work. The father gathers food for her. Birds work hard at protecting their eggs. They do this until the eggs are ready to hatch. Once the chicks break out of their shells, they still depend on their parents for food. When they are hungry, they cry until their mother or father drops some food in their open mouths. Bird parents spend most of their day looking for food to feed to their young.

Reptile eggs are different from bird eggs. Bird eggs are hard and mostly smooth. Most reptile eggs are soft and leathery. They are not always perfectly round or oval. Most snakes and lizards find a nice patch of dirt

*The female Blandings sea turtle lays her eggs in the
sand and then covers them for protection.*

or sand when it is time to lay their eggs. They dig a hole and drop the eggs

in. A group of reptile eggs is called a **clutch**. After laying the eggs, the reptile

will cover them with dirt or sand. This hides them from hungry predators. It

also helps keep them warm. Once this job is done, the mother will leave. She

will not come back. Reptiles are born with all of the basic skills they need to

survive. This is a good thing because once they hatch, those baby snakes or

lizards are on their own.

REAL WORLD SCIENCE CHALLENGE

Human mothers are pregnant, or carry their babies inside their bodies, for nine months. Kangaroo babies only grow inside their mother's body for a short time. Once they're born, they crawl into her pouch and finish growing there. Which of the following animals do you think has the longest pregnancy?

- Wolf
- Gorilla
- Elephant
- Tiger

(Turn to page 29 for the answer)

This is different from mammals and birds. Most mammals spend a lot of time with their young. They often stay with them for several years.

Unlike reptiles, mammals are not born with many survival skills. They need to learn these skills from their parents. Tiger cubs watch their mother hunt for several months before they try to help out. They don't have the skills to hunt on their own until they reach two years of age.

Primates, like baboons, live in large family groups. They spend most of their childhood learning the right ways to act in the group. This is an important skill. Without it, they will be kicked out or forced to live on the edge of the group. Life without a family group is very hard for a baboon.

Some insects have a very different kind of life cycle. They lay eggs. But the baby that hatches looks completely different from the parent. Butterfly eggs, for instance, hatch into caterpillars. This wormlike stage of life is

A family of baboons keeps watch on the rocks. Baby baboons learn social skills from the adults in their family group.

A brightly colored caterpillar is in its larval stage after hatching. Soon it will become a butterfly.

called the larval stage. The young **larva** eats lots of food and grows very large. Then it builds a cocoon, or a shell, around itself. Inside, it changes into an adult. When the cocoon opens, a full-grown butterfly comes out.

More than 1 million different species of animals share the earth. Each one has a different way of living, eating, and raising its young. The more you read and learn about animals, the more you will discover how amazing and unique they really are!

REAL WORLD SCIENCE CHALLENGE ANSWERS

Chapter One
Page 5

- The iguana is a reptile. All lizards are reptiles. They have scales and shed their skin as they grow.
- A great white shark is a fish. It has gills and can breathe underwater.
- Chickens are birds. They have feathers and beaks. Chickens are not very good fliers though. They can only fly up into the lower branches of a tree or the rafters in a barn.
- Bats fly, so many people think they are birds. They are not. Bats are mammals. They have fur and nurse their young with milk.
- A tree frog is an amphibian. When it hatches from an egg, it has a tail and breathes underwater. When it becomes an adult, it grows legs and begins to breathe air.

Chapter Two
Page 11

The longer you watch, the more you will see. In a pond, you might see fish, frogs, turtles, and even birds. The fish need water to live. So do the turtles and frogs. The birds depend on those other animals for their food. In a tree, you might see a squirrel, some birds, and a caterpillar. The squirrel finds shelter and safety in the treetop. The birds may make their nest in the branches. Caterpillars love trees because they love to eat the tasty leaves.

Chapter Three
Page 22

Predators often have sharp teeth and strong jaws. They use these to catch their prey and hold on to it. Most predators also have eyes that face forward. This helps them focus on their prey.

Many prey animals have camouflage. This means the color of their fur, feathers, or skin helps them blend into their surroundings. If the predator can't see them, it can't catch them!

Chapter Four
Page 26

The elephant wins the prize for the longest pregnancy. Elephant mothers are pregnant for twenty-two months. That is almost two years!

GLOSSARY

adaptations (a-dap-TAY-shuns) features of living organisms that help them survive in their habitat

carnivores (CAR-ni-vohrs) animals that eat only other animals

cartilage (CAR-tuh-lidj) firm but flexible type of tissue in animals' bodies

clutch (KLUHCH) collection of bird or reptile eggs

ecosystem (EEK-oh-sis-tem) type of habitat that includes all the animals, plants, land, water sources, and even weather patterns that make it up

food chain (FOOD CHANE) cycle in which one life form eats another

gills (GILS) organ which allows underwater animals to get oxygen from water

habitat (HA-buh-tat) place where an animal lives

herbivores (UR-bi-vohr) animals that eat only plants

larva (LAR-VUH) pre-adult stage of some insects

molting (MULTing) losing skin or feathers to make room for new growth

omnivores (AHM-ni-vore) animals that eat both plants and animals

predator (PRED-a-tohr) animal that hunts and kills other animals for food

prey (PRAY) animal that is being hunted by a predator

species (SPEE-sheez) group of animals who share common physical features and behaviors

tundra (TUN-druh) vast, flat, treeless part of the Arctic where soil just below the surface is always frozen

FOR MORE INFORMATION

Books

Burnie, David. *Animal: The Definitive Visual Guide to the World's Wildlife.*
New York: DK, 2005.

McKay, George. *The Encyclopedia of Animals: A Complete Visual Guide.*
Berkeley and Los Angeles: University of California Press, 2004.

Strauss, Rochelle. *Tree of Life: The Incredible Biodiversity of Life on Earth.*
Tonawanda, NY: Kids Can Press, 2004.

Web Sites

National Geographic Animal Facts and Information
http://animals.nationalgeographic.com/animals
A thorough collection of animal facts, articles, and videos.

PBS's *Nature* Critter Guide
http://www.pbs.org/wnet/nature/critter.html
A list of fun and informative facts from the award-winning
PBS television series *Nature*.

San Diego Zoo Animal Bytes
http://www.sandiegozoo.org/animalbytes/index.html
An interactive Web site of animal information, sounds, videos, and more from
the world-famous San Diego Zoo.

Wild Animals A to Z
http://animal.discovery.com/wild-planet/animals.html
Animal Planet's online animal information resource.

INDEX

ABOUT THE AUTHOR

Stuart P. Levine has written a number of books about animals and wildlife. He has worked as an animal keeper and trainer for exotic animals in several zoos and spent time researching primate behavior in Central America. Currently he works as a wildlife educator in an animal park in central Florida.